The Cardozo Kindersley Workshop

A GUIDE TO COMMISSIONING WORK

The Cardozo Kindersley Workshop

A GUIDE TO COMMISSIONING WORK

by Lida Lopes Cardozo Kindersley

CARDOZO KINDERSLEY   CAMBRIDGE 2003

This book is for David, to whom my life and work are dedicated, and in memory of John Dreyfus.

Preface by John Dreyfus (1918–2002)

David Kindersley became my friend shortly after he set up his workshop near Cambridge in 1946. We shared a passion for letterforms: I as a printer, David as a letter-cutter and designer. He had learnt his skills between 1934 and 1936 as an apprentice in Eric Gill's workshop. Unlike most of the other apprentices, David's personality and ambition were strong enough for him to be able to develop his own style very quickly and to gain his independence; but he kept a deep respect for Gill's ideals and teaching.

During our long friendship, I was fascinated to observe how much his style of drawing and arranging letters was affected by new influences, notably while working for several months in Los Angeles during 1967 as a Senior Research Fellow in the University of California. In his later years he worked so closely with Lida Lopes Cardozo (who joined his workshop over twenty years ago) that I was often unsure whose hands had been responsible for the letters I admired in the workshop's output. Perhaps that is the best compliment I can pay to the ethos of a lettering workshop.

Much to my delight, David twice carried out commissions for me. But if we had not already been friends before the work began, I should have found it a great help to have read an account of how his workshop operated. This has now been capably written by Lida, his widow, for the benefit of those with only a vague idea of how the work-

shop continues to be run. Lida also explains, visually and verbally, how it can turn a patron's tentative ideas into a joyous example of imaginative craftsmanship.

The variety and vitality of the objects created in the workshop have added importantly to the attractiveness of many public buildings and spaces where the work can already be admired. Now I hope that Lida's explanations of the workshop's methods and practice will lead to the execution of many new commissions. For these will certainly add to the public's enjoyment of the several arts which combine to create the loveliest monumental inscriptions.

London, October 1996

One of the commissions cut in slate for John Dreyfus

Contents

The workshop tradition

We are a workshop, following a tradition that has come down to us through the Arts and Crafts movement, via Eric Gill to David Kindersley, who started this workshop in 1946.

It is a workshop in every sense: a place where craftsmen and women work; where creative and experimental work is done; and, above all, where people work together, for together we are more than we could be separately.

We continue to take on apprentices, handing the tradition on, as it was handed on to us. We do not see our work simply as a technique, though technically it must be perfect. Through our love for letters – for the alphabet, for writing and lettering – we aim for perfection in the transmission of meaning. It is our reason for being.

We do not work in isolation, therefore. We need clients to generate ideas and to share ideals; the things we make must be useful as well as beautiful. As David Kindersley said, "the workshop should be a living organism and if it isn't, its further existence is pointless".

The workshop is run by Lida Lopes Cardozo. Lida was born in Holland, and trained originally at the Royal Academy in The Hague with Gerrit Noordzij. She joined David Kindersley as an apprentice, running the workshop with him from 1976. As the workshop flourished, so did

The workshop today (left to right from top):
Fergus Wessel, Sarah Charlesworth, Paul Kindersley, Vincent Kindersley,
Graham Cannon, Annika Larsson, Jean Moxon, Noel Cribb,
Hallam Kindersley, Lida Lopes Cardozo Kindersley, Graham Beck and
Emi Sato

Lida and David's partnership. They married and had three sons, and continued to work closely together. Since David's death in 1995 the workshop has continued in Lida's hands.

There are usually three or four other letter cutters and carvers in the workshop. Young (and sometimes not so young) people come to learn and work with us. Teaching is a vital part of workshop life.

We cut with hammer and chisel, and avoid using machines. Indeed, oil and stone are very bad companions. As machinery inevitably involves noise, dirt and maintenance, we prefer to depend on our own hands. We design, cut, paint, gild, and fix all our own work. We do have a few things that plug in: a grinding wheel for shaping our chisels, a drill, a jigsaw, lights and, of course, the kettle.

Our coffee and tea breaks are good times to start a visit. When you do come, you will enter a quiet workshop with a disciplined way of working. You will hear the distinctive and characteristic sound of hammer on chisel, and you will be welcome.

Every job is different and every need specific, so the result will be original and unexpected every time. However, there is a definite discipline with certain steps to follow when working with stone, wood or indeed any material.

We have fifty years' experience of going through this process. In this booklet we should like to show you how we can work together so that little by little we will come from your first idea to an end result.

First idea to end result

The first step

On first approaching us, some people have a clear idea of what is needed, while others may not know how to put their ideas into words, or even what would be possible.

You may be thinking about a headstone, memorial plaque or commemorative inscription, sundial or birdbath, quotation or alphabet, heraldry, or anything else: a bookplate or a letterhead, engraved glass or carving.

The best thing at this early stage is to meet us in the workshop. Here we have a lot of material to stimulate our initial discussions. You can see work in progress as well as work completed, and look at different materials. If you cannot visit us, do write, because we can work from text and, because the location is important, from a photograph.

We can also come to you or to the site, which is something we like to do anyway, particularly when we are considering a sundial or something that is to be fixed to a building, either inside or outside. It is amazing how much information can be gleaned from a good look at the location, its position and lighting, and how much this helps to decide matters of style and material.

Glass paper-weight with flourished alphabet

A B C D E
a b c d e f g h i j k
F G H I J K
l m n o p q r s t u
L M N O P
v w x y z & æ œ
Q R S T U
1 2 3 4 5 6 7 8 9 0
V W X Y Z

What we need to know from you

During your visit to the workshop there are some questions you can expect from us. We will not need to have all the answers immediately, but it is good to be prepared.

The object **What kind of thing needs to be made?**

The occasion **What is being celebrated or commemorated?**

Time constraints **Is there a completion date for an anniversary or an event?**

The text **What needs to be said?**

The location **Where and in what position?**

Welsh slate 'Whatnot' painted off-white

What you need to know from us

There are questions we shall expect from you, although we shall probably not have all the answers before we have discussed the plans with you in detail. Ask whatever you want to know; we are happy to discuss anything.

How much? *The costs are directly related to the amount of work involved in making the object. We charge by the day, so until we know what we are going to do it is difficult to say whether a headstone, for example, would be two or five thousand pounds. It all depends on the size, the mat-erial, the amount of text to be cut, the carving and so on.*

How long? *Working on stone is a slow business. The time from the start of a commission to its completion depends on the amount of work to be done. Something small can take weeks; something large, months.*

The more we all put in, the more comes out. The more we can find out from each other, the better the work will be.

Street names throughout Great Britain and the Commonwealth use David Kindersley's lettering. We can design a new typeface for a specific need.

Design

Our work has to stand the test of time. We must be very careful to concentrate on the perfect transmission of meaning. To begin with we focus on specific design decisions:

1 Material Among other considerations, we look at materials in relation to the environment of the finished object.

2 Size and shape This will depend on the constraints of the material or the site, and the requirements of the text, as well as the choice of words and their division into lines.

3 Type of lettering The choice of letterforms, weight and size, letter spacing, interlinear spacing and punctuation.

4 Embellishments The use of colour, texture or gilding.

We go through these matters step by step to develop a feel for what is needed: something disciplined and stern, something frivolous and free, something traditional, something experimental. We have no qualms about being either derivative and traditional, or experimental and innovative.

The design is guided by a clear understanding of what you want and by our own ground rules: that the work should fit its purpose and surroundings; that we strive to achieve technical perfection; that discipline is inherent in all aspects of the work; that the triangular relationship of material, artist and patron is celebrated by us all, working together from beginning to end; and that as the work develops, so do we.

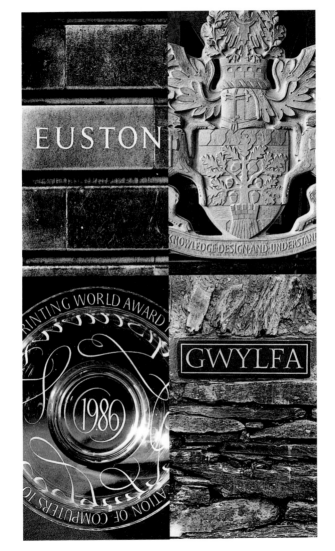

Estimating time and cost

Once we have looked through all the possibilities, discussed as much as is necessary and seen whatever we need to see, we make a sketch. Normally, a sketch will be sent to you within two to four weeks of our meeting. If time is short, we can send it sooner.

Depending on the complexities of the design, we may need to do some research before preparing the sketch. Since we live and work in Cambridge we have a close link with the University and can call on many specialists for information. We always consult experts for inscriptions in Latin, Greek and Hebrew, and for all other scripts too, such as Japanese, Arabic and Cyrillic.

We also ask for expert advice when we need to calibrate a sundial or work with heraldry, or when we want specific geological knowledge for particular kinds of stone.

With the small sketch, we produce details of costs and a time-scale. At any one time we are working on several commissions, and sometimes we are involved in training a new apprentice as well, so we have to be realistic in our time estimates. There are, of course, some dates that have to be met and we do always meet them.

At this stage, the sketch is still open to discussion and revision. If there is anything you are unsure of, this is the moment to mention it.

ΟΥΜΕΝΓΑΡΤΟΥΓΕΚΡ
ΕΙΣΣΟΝΚΑΙΑΡΕΙΟΝ
ΗΟΘΟΜΟΦΡΟΝΕΟΝΤΕ
ΝΟΗΜΑΣΙΝΟΙΚΟΝΕΧ
ΗΤΟΝΑΝΗΡΗΔΕΓΥΝΗ

Odyssey VI 182–4

ואשתו
גרדה יכבד
בתר אתרי עקב

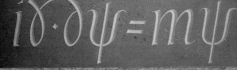

$$i\vartheta \cdot \partial\psi = m\psi$$

DOMINIC·SCHOLA·SERViTII

Permits and faculties

For most headstones a permit approving the design is required. A churchyard might have restrictions for materials and size. It is a good idea first to consult the rector or vicar.

A faculty is granted by the church authorities for something that falls outside their standard rules. A faculty is always required for a memorial inside a church. It can sometimes take months to come through.

The rector or vicar can advise on how to approach the Parochial Church Council (PCC), the Diocesan Advisory Committee (DAC) and the Diocesan Registrar, who will pass the papers on to the Chancellor for him to grant the faculty.

Work in public places

Planning permission from the local authority is usually needed for sculpture or inscriptions to be put in a public place. Wall-plates and wall sundials do not need permission unless they are put on a listed building.

We can help by approaching the authorities on your behalf, if you prefer.

IN MEMORIAM
RICARDI HENRICI
LOVELOCK LEE
HVIVS DOMVS
SCHOLARIS
QVI OBIIT AD
MDCCCCXLVIII

HENRY
DONOVAN
ANGUS
PENNELLS
1926-1993
*a loving man
beloved
by his wife*
JOY ALICE
MAY

and their family

Sketch and go-ahead

The scale sketch we send to you will give the following information:

the size and shape of the object;

the material and thickness;

the combination of letterforms and flourishes;

an indication of symbols, heraldry, reliefs etc;

and the positioning of the object.

Even if you are entirely happy with the sketch, there are three things you need to do before we start cutting:

1 Check everything At this stage it is vital to check everything with everyone concerned: the dates, spelling, titles and so on. The sketch is open to correction. Mistakes on paper can easily be put right, but once the stone is cut, it is a different matter.

2 Apply for permit The design may need to be cleared for a permit (see Permits and faculties, p18). We can do this for you, and will ask you for the relevant information at the time.

3 Give go-ahead in writing Once the design and estimate are approved by you and by any relevant authorities, we can proceed. At this point we will order the material and may ask for one third of the quoted cost on account.

Drawing on to the stone

The first thing to be done after receiving the material in the workshop is to shape it. After that, we draw out the design on the stone.

At the moment of drawing on to the stone, our attention is completely focused on making the design work. We draw from a scale sketch, not from a full-size drawing. We would miss an opportunity to improve if we were merely to transfer a full-size drawing on to the stone. The drawing out is a vital step; it is where the sketch develops. As we face the stone we need to bring all our senses to bear on it and be completely open so that we can make the right decisions.

At this stage we welcome anyone who would like to come and look before cutting starts. In fact, we love this moment and very much want to share it. If any questions arise at this stage, we are happy to discuss them. Anything you contribute adds to the finished work.

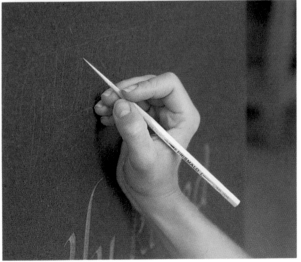

Cutting

It is during the cutting that we make the final decisions about the precise letterform, its depth and its spacing. Bad spacing ruins a good design.

Cutting is a quiet and solitary business. This act is our moment of meditation and concentration. All our attention must be on the tip of the chisel.

However, we do not mind an audience at this stage. In fact, we are quite used to it as we often cut work in situ. Working in Westminster Abbey or Canterbury Cathedral invites constant comments, and when deep in concentration we do not hear them. When we do hear a question, we know that it is time for a break anyway.

Mistakes

Mistakes should be avoided through vigilant checking by all concerned. We recommend asking a third party not directly involved to check the scale sketch. We ourselves check rigorously at every stage.

Though mistakes do not often occur, it has happened that, for example, incorrect dates have been cut. When this happens, there are a number of things we can do:

1 Re-cut It is always the best solution to start afresh. If the mistake were ours this is what we would do.

2 Rubbing out This means chiselling down and rubbing smooth a large area around the mistake. This takes some time, it is much quicker and cheaper than re-cutting the whole inscription but eventually will show up.

3 Filling On the whole we are against this, particularly on outdoor inscriptions. We can make it look good, but the filling will not weather in the same way as the stone, and time will tell.

Rectified mistakes will always show and are much better avoided.

Decoration

Sometimes the contrast between a stone's surface and the newly cut letterforms or the carving can be rather weak. Quite often we paint the letters to help the inscription show up for the first few years. With slate we tend to paint the letters off-white to re-create the freshly cut contrast. They can of course be painted any colour, or even gilded.

We use real gold leaf, and platinum leaf for a silver colour. (Because we do not varnish metals, silver itself would go black.) Heraldry is usually painted and gilded. We use sign-writers' paint and only a little varnish. This means that the paint does not peel off but slowly weathers away.

On wood, brick or porous limestone we can use a stain (a thin wash of colour) rather than paint.

Fixing

We prefer to fix our work into position ourselves. It can be hard work, but it gets us out and about to see the places where our work belongs. It is exciting to see the finished work in situ. This is a special moment for us all, seeing the realisation of the idea behind a commission; and, as David wrote in 'Letters Slate Cut', fixing is always fun.*

There are four different kinds of fixing:

1 *A permanent wall fixing*
2 *A wall fixing that can be removed*
3 *An upright stone fixed into the ground*
4 *A ledger stone fixed flat on the ground*

Keyhole plates are sunk into the back so that an inscription can be hung on screws and can therefore be moved.

Wall fixings are always invisible, except for brass plaques which are screwed in at the front. Permanent fixings can require special building skills, especially fixings in flint churches, old stone walls and glass or wooden panelling.

* *'Letters Slate Cut', published by Cardozo Kindersley in 1990, explains our working methods in detail and shows many examples of our work.*

Records

When the work is finished – cut, painted and ready to go – we always make both a photograph and a rubbing for our records. The photograph shows the object. The rubbing gives us detailed information about the size of letters and their spacing, the thickness of strokes, precise interlinear space, margins and letterforms. We could even reconstruct the work from it if necessary.

We have an enormous archive of things of different shapes and sizes. We also keep all our correspondence, and have files in the workshop going back to 1936 when David left Eric Gill and started out on his own.

Flourishes

Many people love flourishes and so do we. They are some-times useful and always decorative. They can be there to emphasise meaning, to fill a space, to make a strong design form, or for the joy of decoration.

Flourishes have their own spring and strength. Calligra-phically their weight has a direction, so it is more natural to flourish off italics rather than capitals, but, as stone cutters, we can manipulate them for our own ends. A flourish should never become a mass of spaghetti.

Symbols

There is sometimes a need or a desire for symbols to be carved. Traditional symbols have many varieties. Here are a few examples of forms of a cross.

Latin   Greek   Maltese   St Andrew's

A carving can also be used to symbolise an aspect of a person's life: a place, career or nickname, for instance. Or, as shown here, a favourite animal or interest.

Heraldry

Heraldry in full colour always enlivens a monument. When we are asked to incorporate heraldry into a design, we need to have a written description or pictorial representation of the armorial bearings. It helps if we can see an example.

We check all heraldry both with the heraldic authorities and with our own expert.

Reliefs

A symbol, motto, heraldry or any other design can be cut in three ways: in the round, relief or sunk relief. The effects are quite different.

In the round The sculptural approach.

Relief All of the stone surrounding the image is cut away and the carving is left proud.

Sunk relief Only a part of the immediately surrounding material is cut away, usually in a regular shape. Sunk relief takes less time, since much less stone is cut away, and it is therefore cheaper. It also gives more protection to the image, which lies below the surface of the stone.